The Sinking of the *General Slocum*: The History of New York City's Deadliest
Maritime Disaster

By Charles River Editors

About Charles River Editors

Charles River Editors provides superior editing and original writing services across the digital publishing industry, with the expertise to create digital content for publishers across a vast range of subject matter. In addition to providing original digital content for third party publishers, we also republish civilization's greatest literary works, bringing them to new generations of readers via ebooks.

Sign up here to receive updates about free books as we publish them, and visit Our Kindle Author Page to browse today's free promotions and our most recently published Kindle titles.

Introduction

The Sinking of the General Slocum (June 15, 1904)

"There were scenes of horror on the General Slocum and on shore such as it would not be decent to set down on paper…" – J.S. Ogilvie, *History of the General Slocum disaster by which nearly 1200 lives were lost by the burning of the steamer General Slocum in Hell gate, New York harbor, June 15, 1904* (1904)

There is a popular saying that declares "timing is everything," and in no other field of study is that truer than in history. For instance, under normal conditions, a ship that sank with more than 1,000 passengers aboard – most of whom died – would be big news, yet today the sinking of the PS *General Slocum* is often overlooked if not entirely forgotten. While it might have generated the type of publicity and reaction of the Johnstown Flood of 1889 or the Galveston Hurricane of 1900 under normal circumstances, deadliest disaster in New York City's history before 9/11, and the second deadliest maritime disaster in peacetime in American history has become something of a historical footnote.

On June 15, 1904, an annual gala was held on the passenger ship as it steamed up the East River, with about 1,400 people from St. Mark's Evangelical Lutheran Church. Consisting mostly of German immigrants, the boat was packed with women and children, and when a small fire started on the ship shortly after the trip began, faulty equipment was unable to put it out or stop it from spreading. On top of that, the lifeboats were tied up and the crew, which never conducted emergency drills, was unprepared for a potential disaster. When parents put life preservers on their children and then had them enter the water, they soon learned that the life preservers were also faulty and didn't float.

As the disaster unfolded, over 1,000 passengers burned to death or drowned, many swept under the water by the East River's current and weighed down by heavy wool clothing. Few people on board knew how to swim, exacerbating the situation, and eventually the overcrowded decks began to collapse, crushing some unfortunate victims.

In the end, the *General Slocum* sank in shallow water while hundreds of corpses drifted ashore, and the fallout was immediate. The captain was indicted for criminal negligence and manslaughter, and the ship's owner was also charged. While the captain would receive a 10 year sentence, the company in charge of the *General Slocum* got off with a light fine. In a somewhat fitting postscript, the ship was salvaged and converted into a barge, only to sink once again during a heavy storm in 1911.

It is said that time heals all wounds, but in the case of the *Slocum* disaster, the wounds weren't so much healed as overshadowed. The Triangle Shirtwaist Factory fire took over 100 lives in New York City in 1911 and led to calls for serious workplace reforms, and a few years later, World War I began in Europe. With that, much of the sympathy Americans previously felt for the loss of over 1,000 German lives on the *Slocum* evaporated.

The Sinking of the General Slocum: The History of New York City's Deadliest Maritime Disaster chronicles the fateful chain of events that led to one of the worst tragedies in American history. Along with pictures of important people, places, and events, you will learn about the *General Slocum* like never before, in no time at all.

The Sinking of the *General Slocum*: The History of New York City's Deadliest Maritime Disaster

About Charles River Editors

Introduction

Chapter 1: As Fine a Day for a Picnic as Ever Was

Promotional material for the *General Slocum*

"There were several hundred excursionists already on the pier when the Slocum arrived. There were mothers full of pride in their lusty German-American babies, and full of anxiety for fear some of them would fall overboard in their haste to get on board the Slocum before anybody else did. A band came and went to the after deck and began booming out melodies dear to the German and the East Side heart. The mothers and children kept pouring across the gang plank and scurrying for "good places" about the decks. The Rev. G. C. F. Haas, and his assistant, the Rev. J. S. Schultz, stood on opposite sides of the gang plank and welcomed the mothers and the scholars. Policeman [Charles] Kelk and [Abel] Van Tassel, full of experience in the handling of Sunday School excursions, took posts on the off-shore side of the steamer, ready to dive after any towhead who by mischance should fall overboard. It was as fine a day for a picnic as ever was. The sunlight made the blue water seem as bright as though it lay anywhere but between the piers of the biggest city of this nation. ... Pastor Haas was good-natured, and it was well along toward 10 o'clock when the Slocum started, the band on the upper deck playing 'Ein Feste Burg 1st Unser Gott.'" – J.S. Ogilvie, *History of the General Slocum disaster by which nearly 1200 lives were lost by the burning of the steamer General Slocum in Hell gate, New York harbor,*

June 15, 1904 (1904)

It should have been a perfect day, the kind that the German immigrant families would look back on in years to come with delight and nostalgia. June 15, 1904 was a warm, mild day in New York City. Spring had begun to give way to summer and the trees and flowers around the harbor were in full bloom. Families from St. Mark's Evangelical Lutheran Church arrived at the pier early that morning, the women in their best dresses and shading their faces with parasols while the few men that had been able to miss work that day talked politics, well assured that New York's own Theodore Roosevelt would win reelection in the fall. Little children ran from each other and played tag while their older siblings tried to talk without being interrupted. There were over 1,400 people there that day, all from one of New York City's largest churches, and most of its members had turned out for their 17th annual excursion on the mighty passenger steamship PS *General Slocum*. As the Reverend George Hass raised his arms for attention and led his congregation in a rousing version of "Ein Feste Burg ist Unser Gott" (A Mighty Fortress is Our God), he had no way of knowing that within just a few hours, almost everyone on board that day would be dead, victims of the second deadliest maritime disaster in American history and the worst tragedy in New York City's history until the attacks on September 11, 2001.

Pictures of St. Mark's Evangelical Lutheran Church (now Community Synagogue Max D. Raiskin Center)

As the ship pulled away from the dock at 9:40 and the band played rousing tunes, Hass assured people on board, "I have worked hard to make this better than any excursion we have had before." They were heading for Locust Grove on Long Island for the church's popular annual picnic, and hampers of food were piled on the deck, as aromas of sausage and sauerkraut filled the air. Haas felt particularly blessed to have secured the *General Slocum* since it was considered one of the best ships plying the Manhattan at that time. The ship's captain, George Van Schaick, was famous for having survived the loss of the *Portland* when it broke in two during an 1898 blizzard, and he was also looking forward to an easy, pleasant day undisturbed by any significant problems.

General Slocum token in the collection at The Mariners Museum

Van Schaick

The *General Slocum* was still a relatively new ship, having been built by the Knickerbocker Steamer Company in 1891, but she was old enough to have been well run in and had more than a decade's worth of experience plying the waters around New York. According to a report written shortly after the accident, "The *General Slocum* was one of the best known vessels about New York Harbor. Since the time of her launching, in 1891, she has been employed in so many different capacities, and on so many different runs, that possibly five out of every ten people in New York City have, at some time, been aboard of her, or have seen her at close range. Built for the Rockaway service as sister ship to the Grand Republic, she was kept on that run during most of the days of the summer months, and during the thirteen years she has been in the service she has carried to that resort almost enough people to equal the population of this city. As an excursion boat she was easily one of the most popular of all the vessels that ply the surrounding waters. Her build did not permit of much room for dancing, but the younger folks usually found room in a rather small space on the main deck for this amusement, while the general arrangement of the vessel, with corners and spaces to suit every kind and class, gave her great popularity. During the excursion season, which comes before and after the Rockaway season, she was employed almost every day by excursion parties."

The report went on to praise the ship, which was said to have been a "boat builder's dream," adding, "[S]he was said to be unsinkable. … She was a sidewheel boat, each wheel 31 feet in diameter, bearing 26 paddles. She had a steam, steering gear of the latest pattern, and was lighted by 250 electric lights. She had a speed of about 18 miles an hour. The General Slocum had three decks, the main deck provided aft with a comfortable and roomy cabin for women, and with a restaurant forward. The next above, the promenade, held the main cabin, richly lined with highly polished sycamore and upholstered in red velvet. Forward and aft of this cabin were roomy deck spaces. The band usually played on the after-part of this deck. The hurricane deck was provided with a running bench all along the outside. Her two funnels were almost amidships and were placed one on each side. Her body was painted white, and her funnels a medium yellow, while her name in large gold letters stood out on either side. She carried a crew of 22 men, a captain and two pilots."

However, there was a darker side to the *General Slocum*'s history, one that most of those on board that day did not know. The report noted, "The *General Slocum* has been in almost constant misfortune since a time shortly after her launching. No other vessel in the harbor has nearly as long a record of accidents as she, and she has cost her owners thousands of dollars at various times for repairs and for hauling her off some bar on which she had lodged. … The officers of the Knickerbocker Steamboat Company have frequently been up before the authorities for over-crowding the Slocum. Almost every year special men were detailed to watch her, and charges against her were often made. In 1895 the company was fined $1,670 for a violation."

There were other problems as well, and they would tragically become all too apparent that afternoon. Although the ship had recently passed inspection, much of her equipment was in shocking disrepair, neglected by the Knickerbocker Steamboat Company and overlooked by the crew.

Nevertheless, as the ship pulled away from the dock, many standing on shore watched enviously, wishing they were also on board and heading for a day of games and good food.

Chapter 2: Real Danger

"Though Capt. Van Schaick did not know it, the steamer must even then have been on fire. Just back of the crew's quarters, up in the bow of the steamer under the main deck, is what is called the second cabin. On the *Slocum* this cabin has been used as a sort of storeroom. Spare hawsers and paint and oils were kept there. Gasoline was kept there, and it was there that Albert Payne, a negro steward, kept the ship's lamps when they were not in place, and cleaned and filled them.

Payne, his face ashy with the horrors he had been through, swore that he had finished cleaning all the lamps before the boat left her dock early that morning, and that he had not been in the room, except to see that everything was all right. He swore that just before the boat left East Third street the second cabin was all right. Along the Astoria shore, where there are many yards for the building of small boats, the trouble was known sooner than it was on the steamer itself. …it was quite a while after the Slocum was first found to be on fire that the seriousness of the situation was understood by all of her officers and crew. Very few of the passengers knew anything of the real danger they were in until the burning and drowning had begun." – J.S. Ogilvie, *History of the General Slocum disaster by which nearly 1200 lives were lost by the burning of the steamer General Slocum in Hell gate, New York harbor, June 15, 1904* (1904)

Disaster didn't take long to strike, because the *Slocum* had traveled less than half a mile when it became obvious that something was very wrong. William Alloway, the captain of a nearby dredge, notice a sudden burst of smoke coming from the lower deck of the ship, just in front of the smokestacks, so he sounded his whistle in an attempt to get the *Slocum*'s attention. Other boats also began to sound warnings, which alarmed people on board. Clara Stuer, one of the passengers, described the initial confusion: "I was sitting on the upper deck with Miss Millie Mannheimer, 40 years old; Miss Lillie Mannheimer, her niece, 9 years old, and Walter, the latter's brother, aged 11. We had just passed the entrance to the Harlem River, and were going slowly when Lillie called to her aunt, saying: 'I think the boat is on fire, auntie; see all the smoke.' 'Hush!' replied her aunt, 'you must not talk so. You may create a panic' Lillie would not be silenced, however, and it seemed but a few moments later when there was a roar as though a cannon had been shot off, and the entire bow of the boat was one sheet of flames. The people rushed pell-mell over one another, and in the rush I lost track of my friends."

Another child, a little boy, told the newly hired crewman John Coakley that he smelled smoke in a stairwell. Going to inspect the situation, Coakley snatched open the door to the ship's lamp room, a space full of oil and other flammable materials. Had he not opened the door, the hay that had been smoldering on the floor, perhaps lit by an errant cigarette or match, might never have turned into a full-fledged blaze, but the moment the oxygen came in, the burning hay turned into a potentially dangerous fire. To make matters worse, Coakley failed to close the door before rushing to get help, which allowed the fire to grow and spread at an alarming rate.

Although it took a few minutes to locate and identify the fire, the crew quickly jumped into action and might have prevented the disaster if the ship had the necessary materials with which to fight the blaze. Instead, the hose, which had not been used or maintained since the ship was launched, burst as soon as water was put through it. The men tried one more hose but found that it was similarly useless.

Van Schaick was informed about the fire approximately seven minutes after it was discovered, and at that point, he faced a critical decision. He could immediately turn the ship towards the shore, which was only a few hundred feet on either side, or he could attempt to reach a known docking place instead of running the ship aground. He later insisted that he feared the ship would be broken up on rocks if he stopped where he was, so he decided to proceed to North Brother Island, located about a mile and a half away.

A picture of North Brother Island in the East River

There was another issue, too, at least according to a contemporary account of the disaster. "It seemed to be the captain's purpose as he came up past 130th street to try to find a berth on The Bronx side of the stream. There are a number of coal and wood yards along there and some factories. Rivermen said that he might well have carried out his plan. The land forces of the Fire Department could have reached him there. But he said that a tug warned him off, telling him that he would only be setting fire to the shore buildings, and would not be helping his people in the least, if he ran in there. ...the *General Slocum*...turned again toward North Brother."

As a result, the captain pushed his engines to the limits and made for the island, but as the ship drove into the wind, it fanned the flames and made them spread faster. It also spread the fire directly towards those who were trapped on the back end of the ship. One account of the disaster explained, "It took Captain Van Schaick only a minute to see that he ought to get his passengers ashore as soon as he could. He determined on the North Shore of North Brother Island. It takes time to read of all these things. It took almost no time at all for them to happen. The yells and screams of the few people who were caught on the decks below the hurricane deck forward were ringing horribly across the water. The roar and crackle of the oil-fed flames shut these screams off from the frightened mass of Sunday School people aft."

WRECK OF THE GEN. SLOCUM, SHOWING BOX SURROUNDING THE PADDLE WHEEL. THE DOOR LEADING INTO THIS BOX WAS BROKEN OPEN AND MANY PERSONS WHO TRIED TO ESCAPE THROUGH IT WERE HURLED TO INSTANT DEATH.

Two policemen, Charles Kelk and Abel Van Tassel, were among the first to spring into action, and they were the only ones aboard with any real training in disasters or crowd control. Kelk subsequently provided a harrowing story: "As I was standing there, a woman came rushing toward me with her skirts in a blaze. There was a baby carriage standing near, in which there was a heavy blanket. I seized the blanket, threw it around the woman and rolled her on the deck until the flames were extinguished. She jumped overboard then, and whether she was saved or not, I do not know."

The two men quickly got the crowd moving toward the afterdecks, as far from the fire as possible, but passengers began to panic as the fire continued to spread. Mothers looking for their children became hysterical, even as Hass attempted to calm the crowd. 14 year old Herman Lembeck later recalled, "I was with my mother, two brothers and two sisters on the hurricane deck. We saw a lot of smoke and flames coming from below and mother got scared. Just then Dr. Haas, the minister, came running up to us. He said it was nothing but some coffee burning and begged us to be calm. He then went off looking for his own family."

After he had found what he believed was a safe place for his own wife and daughter, Reverend Hass spoke to his congregants, trying desperately to make himself heard over the growing bedlam, but sadly, his family would not be safe for long. In the aftermath of the disaster, he explained how he was separated from his family: "When the fire shot up to the top deck and drove the crowd back the panic was terrible. The crush from the forward part of the boat swept those in the rear along. The women and children clung to the railing and stanchions but could not keep their hold. I, with my wife and daughter, were swept along with the rest. In the great crush many women fainted and fell to the deck, to be trampled upon. Little children were knocked down. Mothers with their little boys and girls in their arms would give wild screams and then leap into the water. We could see boats pulling out from the shore by this time, and a faint ray of hope came to us. With my wife and daughter I had been swept over to the rail. I got my wife and daughter out on the rail, and then we went overboard. I was so excited that I don't remember whether we pushed over or jumped. When I struck the water I sank, and when I rose there were scores about me fighting to keep afloat. One by one I saw them sink around me. But I was powerless to do anything. I was holding my wife and daughter up in the water as best I could, almost under the side of the boat, when someone, jumping from the rail directly above me, landed on top of us. My hold was broken and we all went under together. When I came up my wife and child were gone. With a great effort I managed to keep afloat, but my strength was about gone when a man on one of the tugs picked me up."

Chapter 3: The Women and the Children Had No Chance

"There were scenes of horror on the General Slocum and on shore such as it would not be decent to set down on paper, even though any chronicler had the ability. It was a boatload of women and little children. For the last mile, when the steamer, spouting flames high into the air, was shooting swiftly out to the Sound with the tide, people on the shore and on other steamers could see the women and children fluttering over the sides into the water in scores. The river is swift there at flood tide. The waves grab forward at one another with hungry white fingers. A strong man would have but little chance. The women and the children had no chance. There have been heard such stories as often come out after a disaster — stories of cruel selfishness by members of the crew, of cold disregard of the Slocum's distress signals and most evident need by pleasure and business craft in the harbor. In the end came the story that there had been looting of the bodies of the dead. Some of these things were more or less true. But there was a glorious record of self-sacrifice and bravery to be set over against all that was evil or unmanly." – J.S. Ogilvie, *History of the General Slocum disaster by which nearly 1200 lives were lost by the burning of the steamer General Slocum in Hell gate, New York harbor, June 15, 1904* (1904)

J.S. Ogilvie, who wrote a contemporary account in the wake of the disaster, described the horrific scene that continued to unfold as the captain kept the ship moving upriver: "There was a puff like a great cough down in the Slocum's inwards. A red starry cloud of sparks and smoke and flames shot up and the greater part of the superstructure aft plunged forward into the flames.

How many hundreds of lives were snuffed out in that one instant nobody will ever know. Outsiders could see writhing, crawling figures in the burning wreckage, slipping down further and further into the flames until they were gone. …there was a thick clustering of women, all screaming, and boys and girls around the edges of so much of the superstructure as was still standing. At the very back Kelk, the policeman, was standing, catching up some of the smallest children and hurling them out at the decks of the nearest following steamers. Mothers threw their children overboard and leaped after them. When the stanchions burned out and the superstructure fell families were separated. … Now the big steamer, ablaze for more than two-thirds of her 250 feet of length, was rounding the point of North Brother Island. The flames were reaching out for the pilot-house. The door toward the fire was blackened here and there and the paint blisters were bursting with little puffs of fire. But the hundred nurses gathered eagerly on shore waiting a chance to help, saw old man Van Schaick and his pilots at their wheel, straining forward as though by their own physical force they could make the boat go faster."

George Kircher was one of the few on board that day who could swim, so he was able to make it to shore, but he narrowly avoided being crushed to death by the collapsing deck: "We had seats along the rail on the top deck, and we stayed together for a long time, hoping that some boat would come and take us off. The flames started in the front of the boat, and that made the crowd come toward us. It was awful to see them. I saw little children trampled on. Everybody was making for the back of the boat, and behind them seemed to be a big wave of flame. As the crowd from the front got to where we were the railing burst into flame, and then I had to jump. Just as I jumped part of the deck gave way and I saw the people tumbling down into the water through a big hole in the deck."

Meanwhile, as people began to grab the life preservers they knew they would soon need, another drastic problem came to light. One report noted, "On many of the bodies which were recovered were life preservers which seemed to have been perfectly worthless. Assistant District Attorney Garvan's attention was called to a collection of the Slocum's life preservers which had been made by Capt. Jack Wade. These life preservers were covered with such flimsy, rotten stuff that they could be ripped open by a scratch with one's thumbnail. They were filled with ground-up cork instead of with solid chunks which would retain their buoyancy. … There the scene was one of terrible confusion. Shrieking women, with little children clustering about them, were trying to get life preservers and fasten them upon their little ones. The men on the boat did their best to help with the life preservers. These, however, proved in a majority of instances to be death traps. Most of the life preservers were so old that their canvas covering was rotten and their fastenings worthless. Jacob Miller, an officer of the Sunday School, tried seven different life preservers before he found one whose fastening did not crumble and break when he put it about a mother of several small children. Other passengers had the same experience."

In the same vein, following the disaster, the *Brooklyn Eagle* observed, "It was confidence that sent hundreds to their death yesterday — confidence that the *General Slocum* was in trim, well manned, equipped with all the fitments for safety of life and rescue. The merest suspicion of such an awful tragedy as occurred a few yards from our shore would have led to a complete overhauling of the boat, to a test of her steering gear, which is alleged by some to have been at fault; of her fire hose and grenades; to an inspection of her galleys, or lamp room, where the fire is supposed to have started, and certainly to a substitution of real life preservers for the flimsy shams that were removed from the bodies. These life preservers are made of rotten canvas, that can be broken by the finger nail, and filled with powdered cork instead of lumps and sheets of the bark that would have had some floating value. The cords by which they are adjusted are as rotten as the canvas, and came apart in the effort to tie them. Then there were the boats. Little seems to have been accomplished by them. The crowds pressed about them so that only two could be put off, it is said. Yet every craft is supposed to be provided with enough of life rafts and life boats to carry off the complement of passengers and crew in an emergency."

Perhaps because the fire spread so fast, or perhaps because of outright negligence, little to no use was made by the passengers and the crew of the Slocum's lifeboats. Nicholas Belzer explained, "I lost track of my wife some time before the fire broke out, and was sitting on the upper deck when I discovered the ship was on fire. I drew my penknife and tried to cut away one of the lifeboats. I succeeded in severing the ropes, but when I got that far I discovered they were held with wire and were immovable. Seeing I could do nothing, I climbed over the edge and down to the lowest deck. I jumped into the river and swam ashore. The water was filled with floating bodies of those who had been drowned, and I had a hard time from being drowned myself by persons who would cling to me."

Making matters worse, many were caught completely off guard by the blaze and had no time to even try to find a life preserver or a lifeboat. John Eli, a 14 year old teenager on board, said, "My mother and my little brother Paul and I were with a big party from our neighborhood. … When we left the pier the deck was packed so with people you could hardly move. The band was playing, and we were all having a fine time. I was standing with some of the boys…when all of a sudden a big sheet of flame burst up through the furnace-room, right in our faces. My mother's dress and Paul's dress caught fire, and I grabbed them and started to run for the side of the boat. There was an awful panic; I was knocked down in the rush. When I got on my feet I couldn't see my mother and brother anywhere. The whole deck was on fire. I was swept into a corner and held there by the crowd. It seemed to me the people were going over the sides like a waterfall. The captain kept blowing his whistle, and I could see lots of boats coming toward us. I found myself in the water when the Slocum got near the shore, and I was picked up by a man in a gasoline launch. I saw lots of burned bodies floating behind the Slocum. Fishman and Gray jumped overboard and swam ashore. I haven't seen anyone else that was with us."

A picture of bodies that had washed ashore

In fact, the fire occurred so fast that the musicians barely had time to realize what was happening. August Schneider, the coronet player with the ship's band, was working that day and had brought his family aboard for a special outing. He remembered, "We were playing on the upper deck. The band, of which George Maurer was leader, was composed of seven musicians. We were seated in the stern when a whole crowd of people suddenly rushed toward us, shouting and screaming. At least half of them jumped right overboard. It wasn't until a few seconds afterward that we saw the smoke and fire. The wind, luckily, was blowing the flames away from us. I got my family together and told them to stick close to me. I took my little Augusta, 3 years old, on my arm and was just considering the best place for safety when the deck broke and fell with the ruins. I still held my child, but my wife and the other two children were torn away from me, and I didn't see them again, and do not know where they are. I was taken on by rescuers on a tugboat."

Many of the women aboard the *General Slocum* drowned, unable to swim either because they didn't know how or because they were weighted down by heavy dresses and petticoats. One survivor, Mrs. John Hynes, managed to make it and tell her story, but she lost one of her three sons. "I was sitting on the main deck at the stern with my son Frank, these two boys and a friend. When the smoke poured up I tied a life preserver on myself and ran upstairs, the boys having preceded me, to the hurricane deck. There we became separated, and I did not see them again until we met on the shore. I stayed on the ship as long as I could; then I jumped into the water.

There another woman struck me on the shoulder when she jumped. I held her up by the waist until my strength failed, and then let her go. She went down, and when she again came to the surface I grasped her by the hair and swam as well as I could with one hand to the paddle-wheel, where I held her head above water until a colored man swam up and took her from me. I don't know who she was, but I recognized her as a member of the church. I don't know whether she was finally saved. When I was relieved of my burden I saw a rowboat approaching, and swam to it, and was taken ashore. I had been there but a few moments when Theodore swam to the shore near where I was, and a few moments later George was brought to shore on a tug. I do not know what became of Frank. About three weeks ago he broke his leg, and was hardly able to walk. He was taken out for the first time to-day. I fear the worst."

Picture of workers on shore carrying a victim

Chapter 4: Making After Her

"At any rate, the General Slocum, observed now by hundreds of horror-dazed people on both sides of the stream and on the islands, turned again toward North Brother. Steamers and tugs from far down stream were making after her. The Department of Correction boat Massasoit was on the far side of the Brother islands. Her captain lay in wait for the Slocum not knowing through what channel she would come. From downstream came the slim, white Franklin Edson, the Health Department boat. Thence, too, came the sturdy little Wade, with her tough-talking, daredevil, great-hearted little captain. Jack Wade. There came also the tugs Theo and Easy Time, tooting their whistles, headed for the burning steamer. On board the Slocum horror was being piled on horror too fast for anyone to keep track of them. The fire, leaping now high above the framework of the steamer's hog-hack and roaring with a smoky glare of red tongues up thirty feet over the tall brown smokestacks, had begun to scorch the edges of the compact mass of women and children who were crowding back out of its way at the rear end of the boat. The greater number of these people by far were on The Bronx side of the decks. They seemed to feel, poor creatures, that small as their chance for rescue was, when it came it would come from the thickly populated shore rather than from the bleak, rocky, bare spaces on the islands on the starboard side." – J.S. Ogilvie, *History of the General Slocum disaster by which nearly 1200 lives were lost by the burning of the steamer General Slocum in Hell gate, New York harbor, June 15, 1904* (1904)

As other ships and boats in the river saw the *Slocum* was in serious trouble, many tried to rush to her aid. Aware that most of the passengers could not swim, the boats surrounded the burning ship and kept reaching out for as many passengers as possible, but they had to deal with panicking passengers. Bernard Miller, one of the few male passengers aboard that day, recalled, "Myself, my wife and four sons, whose ages were three, six, nine and twelve, were sitting on the first deck when I saw smoke coming up through the deck in great clouds. The people lost their heads. I grabbed life preservers and put them on my wife and children, and helped them over the side of the boat into the water. Then I put one on and went after them, telling them to make for the shore. The youngest child was in my wife's arms. All started for Randall's Island. I started after them, but had not taken more than a half dozen strokes when I was surrounded by a half dozen women, who clung to me and dragged me under. I had all I could do to save myself from being drowned by their frantic efforts to hold on to me. A rowboat came up and took us all on board. When we got to shore I searched for my family, but they were not to be found."

One of the rescue boats on the scene was the *Franklin Edson*, whose captain, Henry Eick, later admitted, "It is difficult to tell what to do in such an emergency as that which confronted us in the Slocum disaster. I had just left the Edson, which had come in at the Board of Health pier, at 132d street, when I heard five whistles from my boat. I was down there in a moment, and as I was going across to the Slocum the engineer yelled up the tube that he had water in three lines of hose. We soon saw that water wasn't needed, but quick work to save lives. Everything in the way of life preservers we had went overboard, and then the heaving lines. Fifty feet was as near as I thought it safe to go, for although the windows of the pilot-house were down in their frames I could hear them crackling, and the paint was blistering on the woodwork. Samuel K. Mills, the engineer, and William Balmer, fireman, did fine work. It was hard work in many cases, for there were several large and heavy women, whose weight was increased by their water-soaked garments. We got all those who came our way. Some may think that we ought to have taken the rescued ashore right away for medical attention, but I considered it best to save as many as we could. I think that we got about twenty-five in all. As to how many lived I don't know yet; ten, I am certain of, anyway. Six died after we got them aboard, although we did what we could to revive them."

Albert Rappaport, who was part of the crew of the *Massasoit*, a Department of Corrections ship, described his rescue efforts: "The first one I got was a boy who clung to me after I got back on board, begging that I would not leave him. He said he did not know where to go, as his mother was drowned. I was clad only in underclothes, and in a struggle to save another boy about thirteen years of age my clothing fell about my feet, and it was with great difficulty that I was able to get within reach of a heaving line."

Nearby tugboats also steamed over in an effort to help. The *Wade*, captained by a man of the same name, as well as the *Theo* and the *Easy Time*, were soon close to the mortally wounded *Slocum* and lending aid, as were two young men in a rowboat. In fact, Thomas Miley and John Kain may have been among the first to notice the disaster and immediately headed forward to help. Miley explained, "Both Kain and I were rowing, with our backs toward the Slocum, when we heard a loud report as if an explosion had occurred. When I looked around a cloud of smoke was hovering above the forward part of the steamboat. It seemed only a few moments until flames leaped up, but it may have been longer, because my companion and I were awestricken by the scenes that followed the explosion. We could see women and children struggling with those in the rear, and in their terror they clung to those closest to them and dragged them into the water. While this was happening the Slocum was being run in toward North Brother Island. She had been only 100 feet or so distant from the island shore when we heard the report, but in making the short trip, a long trail of struggling persons was left in the water. Many of them, I think, had been crushed to death in the panic before they touched the water, and they sank at once from view. In a short time flames burst from other parts of the vessel, and the passengers' panic became more terrific. Over the sides they were swept from the decks in masses."

Freda Gardiner, who was just a child that day, vividly remembered how quickly things on the ship got out of hand, but she also relayed how she was rescued: "We were all laughing, because my aunt had said she was afraid on such a big boat. When the first cry of fire came Aunt Louise told me to hold onto her hand, but the crowd came rushing at us and swept her away from me. A big man picked me up in his arms and held me in front of him, but he couldn't keep his feet. I fell over the rail and when I came up I grabbed a big piece of timber. A man in the water tried to grab hold of me and when he missed me I saw him go down. The rowboat came up just as I was about to let go the log, I was so weak."

George Gray had a similar rescue story: "I was sitting on the rear of the upper deck with Otto Hans…and Albert Greenwall…. We were just passing out of Hell Gate when I smelled fire. I looked toward the front of the boat and saw a big cloud of smoke. Otto, Al and I jumped upon a seat and grabbed life preservers. They were rotten and all the cork came out of them. Women and kids were yelling around us something awful. Just then a big blaze of fire came right up through the center of the boat and the people began to jump overboard. Some of the women threw their babies overboard and then jumped after them. The first tug that reached us was the Director. It was a big boat, and came right up close as we were going toward the island. I jumped on the boat and a lot of people jumped on top of me. Half of them fell back into the water between the tug and the boat. In a minute there were so many on the tug the stern was way down in the water and the bow up in the air. They kept on jumping and slipping off the tug and going down. I got hold of the leg of a little girl who was sliding off, and pulled her back, and then I sat on her to keep her from being pushed overboard. I saw a man on the upper deck of the Slocum throw a baby way out into the river and then jump after her. The baby's hair was all afire. The man went right down. Another man jumped over and grabbed the baby and swam with her to the Director, and was pulled up on to the tug by the captain. The baby was alive, all right."

As these experiences suggest, the tugboats proved vital in saving many lives that day. Gray continued, "When the other tugs came up everybody that was left tried to jump on them, and they jumped on top of one another. Lots of them fell off and were drowned. I saw some girls in the river swimming toward the island. They were picked up by rowboats. I saw two little girls who could swim sink when a big wave made by a tug went over them. The women and kids were crying and yelling so we couldn't hear the men on the tugs, who were waving their arms at us for us not to jump. I saw ten men jump into the river long before the tugs came, and not one of them could swim. They all went down. I thought the Director would sink or turn over when she started for the shore, there was so many on her. When we got off we were taken in wagons to the elevated road."

A picture of people looking for bodies in the river

Nonetheless, in spite of everyone's best efforts, many more lives were lost than saved that day. Bernard Miller told this harrowing tale: "Myself, my wife and four sons, whose ages are 3, 6, 9 and 12 respectively, were sitting on the first deck, when I saw smoke coming up through the deck in great clouds. The people on the boat acted as though they had lost their minds. I grabbed life preservers and after putting them on my wife and children assisted them over the side of the boat into the water. Then I put one on and went after them, telling them to make for the shore. The youngest child was in my wife's arms, and she and the three elder ones started for Randall's Island. I started after them, but had not taken more than half a dozen strokes when I was surrounded by half a dozen women, who clung to me and dragged me under. I had all I could do to save myself from being drowned by their frantic efforts to hold on to me when a rowboat came up and took us all on board. I searched for my family in vain. They were not to be found. We did not go over the side, until we could stand the heat no longer, and I was so long on the boat that I was badly burned about the hands and neck."

Chapter 5: The Rescue Work

"A HOSPITAL for the treatment of contagious diseases would not ordinarily be the place to look for heroism of the spectacular type, but there was enough of it shown at North Brother to give the place a name in history. Everybody took a hand in the rescue work — doctors, nurses, ward helpers, engineers, health inspectors and laborers. Even the tuberculosis patients rendered splendid service when so many of the excursionists were struggling in the water after the burning steamer had been beached. None of the other patients was allowed to assist, but many of them who were on the road to recovery volunteered, and there was much excitement among them. It is estimated that the island people rescued 150 persons from drowning. Commissioner McAdoo, accompanied by his secretary reached the island in the middle of the afternoon on board the police boat Patrol. At that time the lawn at the side of the main hospital was literally covered with corpses, and the police and others were fishing them out at the rate of one a minute. Three dead children, all roped together with toy horse-lines, were brought to the surface at one time. The Commissioner shuddered and raised his hat. Next came a woman with a baby clasped in her arms. The Commissioner raised his hat again." – J.S. Ogilvie, *History of the General Slocum disaster by which nearly 1200 lives were lost by the burning of the steamer General Slocum in Hell gate, New York harbor, June 15, 1904* (1904)

A picture of the facilities on North Brother Island

In the midst of the ongoing chaos, the captain and the crew finally made it to the river's edge, but by that point, the fire had spread completely out of control and there was no hope of saving the vessel or most of its occupants. Moreover, the captain was not able to get as close to shore as he had hoped to, so many of those he had hoped would be able to walk to shore jumped into water still over their heads and drowned. Miley noted, "By this time the shore had been reached and the Slocum had been run in between two small piers. Almost before the end of the footbridge reached the shore the shrieking passengers rushed out on the plank and we saw several persons drop into the water as though pushed from the sides. In a short time those who were uninjured were ashore, but there were some who had been hurt by the struggle for life aboard the burning boat who could not reach the gangplank. Some of the less frightened men rushed back and carried these to safety, but there were many, a tugboat captain told us, who had been hemmed in by the flames on the lower deck. This captain had run his boat alongside and picked up ten bodies and saved two little boys. The tug belonged to the Daley Company. The tug Wade was the first to go to the rescue. My companion and I followed and succeeded in recovering two bodies. One was that of an aged woman, and the other body was that of a boy, about 10 years old. The boy's head was burned and his face was bruised, as though he had been injured before he was forced into the water. About a hundred feet from the Bronx shore was a private yacht, with several persons aboard, but they made no move to help the struggling people."

As the burning *Slocum* reached the edge of the island, the boats that were undertaking rescue efforts were joined by firemen coming from all over the city. When the first truck arrived at the water's edge, it was obvious that the men would be able to do little from the shore, so the *Zophar Mills*, New York City's only fireboat, was called in to assist. According to one report, "She came up the river, screaming, with a voice that outscreamed all the other whistles which were being blown in every factory and yard from which the blazing steamship could be seen."

A sketch of *Zophar Mills*

Seeing that the ship was now more in need of rescue personnel than firefighters, the captain of the *Zophar Mills* pulled into the 138th Street pier and took aboard as many men from the Alexander Avenue Station as he could. One account of the disaster described the scene there: "When the Mills got to the General Slocum, the sight, as described by the firemen, was one never to be forgotten. Fire headquarters was informed of the extent of the disaster, and the fireboat William L. Strong was started for the burning Slocum. The *Abram S. Hewitt*, the Brooklyn fireboat, was ordered to proceed to Seventieth street, where she was met by Deputy Fire Commissioner Thomas W. Churchill, Chief Croker and Secretary Volgenau, who boarded her and were hurried to the place of the disaster. When the Mills got four powerful streams on the Slocum the remnant of the passengers, a hundred or more, were making a last struggle against the flames. They were together on the forward part of the boat, moving back from the onward course of the flames. Men, women and children were huddled on the bow, while those nearest to the flames pushed toward those on the bow. Each instant a human being was pushed from the railing of the boat into the water by the backward sweep of the maddened crowd."

The *Abram S. Hewitt*

A picture of the *General Slocum* on fire and a fireboat trying to douse the flames

Even at this point, J.S. Ogilvie noted that people were still trying to escape the flames on board the *Slocum*: "The great hulk was still burning like a furnace on top of the water. Living men and women were still rolling out from her decks. Hundreds sought shelter from the heat under the paddle-boxes, which seemed slow to burn. In there, among the wet paddle-blades, the rescue boats were filled again and again. ... As fast as dead and living were brought ashore the weaker of the convalescent patients took them and carried them up on the lawn. There was a constantly increasing number of physicians coming over from the mainland, some of them in riverboats. Every burnt woman or child who showed any signs of life was carried into the buildings. The nurses' quarters and the doctors' quarters and the stables and every place that had a roof where cots could be erected was filled — except those in which there were contagious diseases. The dead were laid out in long rows on the grass. The living walked or were carried by them. Heartrending recognitions were there: women throwing themselves on the bodies of their children; children catching at their mothers' hands and begging them to "wake up," and screaming inconsolably when they realized that there would be no waking up."

Clearly, by this time the end was near, as there was little anyone else could do to save anyone. The report continued, "The crew of the Mills reported to Chief Croker on the tragic sight, when the General Slocum careened and went down. Men and women who had been crowded together on the bow of the burning steamer were precipitated into the water, struggling to catch hold of one another, and children could be seen floating away from the burned boat. The Mills steamed as close to the Slocum as she could and picked up those who could be picked up. Boathooks were used, and ropes swung to those in the water by the eager firemen on the Mills. Fire fighters dived to rescue women and children, and not a few of the rescued were landed by the Mills at North Brother Island. Chief Croker and the officials on the Hewitt arrived after the work of the fire had been done. Strewn about the face of the water for thousands of yards in all directions were articles of apparel — hats, capes, boxes which had contained luncheon for the picnickers, larger wooden boxes, burning wood, and here and there a dead body."

Meanwhile, people began to arrive at the scene from up and down the shore. When the owner of a marble works near North Brother Island heard what was happening, he shut down his factory and ordered his workers to go down to the shore, commandeer any vessel they could find, and take it out to rescue people. A nearby hospital also sent down all its nurses, and even some tuberculosis patients. One witness noted, "Delicate-looking young women, in the dainty white uniforms which nurses wear, ran down to the water's brink and waded in up to their necks and formed human chains, along which struggling, half-drowned refugees were passed."

Among the nurses who came to help that day was Pauline Fuetz, an 18 year old who was not satisfied at only being part of a chain. According to the same witness's story, "When Dr. Stewart, the superintendent of the hospital, sounded the alarm, Miss Fuetz was among the first to reach the beach. … Fifty feet away the surface of the water was dotted with the heads of struggling women and children. … 'I am going out to them,' cried Miss Fuetz, hysterically, as she pulled off her shoes and skirts. Several nurses caught hold of the girl and tried to restrain her. 'Let me go,' she cried. 'I can swim; I must go to their rescue.' … Five times she reached the shore with her human burdens. The sixth trip almost proved her last. As she passed close by a woman, who gave no sign of life, the latter's arms suddenly clasped around the girl's neck. Those on the shore saw a short struggle and then both disappeared. They arose again, but Miss Fuetz could not break the woman's hold. Finally she placed her hand under the woman's chin and pushed her off. Before the woman could recover her hold Miss Fuetz had passed around and caught her hair and started to push her toward shore. When they were within a few feet of solid footing the woman suddenly turned and grasped the girl again, both sinking. Soon the girl's body appeared on the surface. Her strength had been exhausted. She was dragged ashore more dead than alive and sent to the hospital." When Fuetz was interviewed later, she would only say, "What could I do? I saw the women and children struggling in the water, and what could I do but go to their rescue? I was after the children. I wanted to save the women, too, but my first resolve was to bring the children ashore. The woman who got me nearly took me down with her. If she hadn't been so excited I would have saved her. It wasn't much to do. I learned to swim at Tisbury Park."

Not all the nurses there that day were medical personnel. Louise Galling was on board the *Slocum* as a baby nurse caring for her employer's young children, and she survived on basic instinct: "I had no thought, of what might happen to me. I had never swum a stroke in my life, and I didn't know the slightest thing about how I should begin. I only knew one thing, and that was that I must save the babies. So I took one in each arm and jumped overboard and kicked out with my feet and held them up as best I could. I did not care whether I could swim or not. I only knew that if I didn't I would not save the children. I struggled on through the water and got to the shore. I didn't know how, and I guess I never will, but I saved the babies."

Unfortunately, there was little else the nurses could do but rescue those floundering in the water, because the vast majority of the victims on the Slocum died before ever reaching shore. Even at this later stage of the disaster, though, there were some cases where skilled treatment or luck prevailed. Clara Stuer described how she was rescued and the horrible scene she encountered afterward: "Hundreds of people jumped overboard. I jumped over the rail and dropped down to the lower deck, when I began to dispense with my clothing so that I would have a better chance in the water. Then I started to climb down the side of the boat when I heard a voice calling to me to hold on a minute. I turned and saw a man standing on the bow of a tug which was approaching. I held on, and was soon taken off with a number of other persons who had been rescued from the boat and from the water. The tug then put into the landing on Randall's Island and after putting the people ashore went out for another trip of rescue. As I left the pier I saw what looked to me [to be] 200 bodies, mostly of women and children, along the shore lying on the ground. Physicians were working over many of them. In the center of one group I saw the Rev. George Haas. Several doctors were doing their best to revive him, and as I stood there he opened his eyes and looked about. … I then searched about for my friends, and after a time I found little Lillie. Beyond being bruised she was all right. How she escaped she does not seem to know. All this time the boat was burning, being surrounded by tugs which were trying to extinguish the flames. Lillie and I then made our way to a boat, which took us over to New York, and we came down to Miss Mannheimer's house…but she had not yet reached home."

On a day marked by dozens of heroic deeds, few compare with those of Charles Schwartz, an 18 year old who risked his life to save 22 victims knowing all the while that his own family members, both his mother and his grandmother, had already perished. "I saw my mother and grandmother. They were floating face downward. I got them both ashore and helped the doctors with them on the lawn. 'It's no use' said the doctors, 'We can't do any-thing for your people, my boy.' I felt as though my heart would break, and then I looked out upon the water and saw that there were yet men, women and children who might be saved. A man came along in a little boat, and I swam out to him and worked with him. I went overboard whenever I could and swam up to people and helped them into the boat. Many of them grabbed at me, but I was able to keep off enough to prevent being dragged down. I felt hands way down in the water holding at my feet. Hands caught me everywhere, and above me was the fire raging and roaring. … If I had been a stronger fellow I might have done a great deal more, but I'm light. I weigh only 123 stripped…too light, don't you think? Hero? Oh, I'm nothing like that. I happened to have the knack of swimming a little better than some other persons and so I thought it was my duty to do the best I could. Besides, I'm not thinking much of that kind of thing with my mother and grandmother lying there in the room. I did all I could for them, but the smoke must have suffocated them before they were in the water."

As hard as it may be to believe, less than 30 minutes passed between the time the *Slocum* caught fire and the last living person was pulled from the water. It took Captain Van Schaick about 10 minutes to reach North Brother Island and another 10 minutes for those still on board to swim to shore or be rescued, or to burn to death or drown.

At first, it seemed like perhaps only a few hundred people had perished, but then the tide changed and the channel began to give up its dead. The dead frequently washed ashore in pairs and trios, with mothers still clinging to children and babies bobbing up to the surface like rubber dolls in a child's bath. Those working on shore were forced to care for the living and place them alongside the dead; there were simply too many bodies to quickly transport to the morgue.

Eventually, the morgue itself was filled up, so bodies were laid out on a pier, awaiting discovery and identification by grieving families. Coffin makers and carpenters were called in from all around the city because there were not enough coffins on hand to bury everyone. They brought their tools and wood to the island and quickly assembled the boxes there. One writer observed, "Throughout the city there is mourning, but the seat of grief is in that section of the lower East Side, centering about St. Mark's Lutheran Church, in East Sixth street. As quickly as the bodies were identified at the Morgue by families or friends they were removed to their homes, and in this section there was scarcely a house without its somber sign of mourning at the door. There were few persons in the streets, which presented the appearance they might have on a quiet Sunday. Life there seemed at a standstill. When the survivors left their houses it was to go to the Morgue or to the church itself, where a bureau of information has been established, to ask for tidings of the missing; for in many families more than one went to death on the General Slocum — in many instances four or five, in some as many as nine from a single household. In a block of sixteen houses, eight were counted with flags draped with crape at half-mast."

Pictures of bodies waiting to be identified

Pictures of victims displayed in their coffins

While the light remained, divers continued to go down and bring up bodies, but eventually, the setting sun delayed their work until the following day. In the meantime, outdoor lights were brought in from around the city and set up so that the doctors and nurses could continue to work until, finally, the last survivor could be moved inside for treatment. The dead remained outside, but they were not alone. Faithful workers toiled through the night to make them presentable for their families, carefully removing jewelry and valuables and placing them in numbers bags so that they could later be claimed.

By the time the sun rose the next morning and brought the summer heat with it, the bodies were ready for their trip to the grave, but even that was overwhelming. According to one report, "The first of the funerals of the dead of the Slocum disaster were held June 17, and the bereaved parish of St. Mark's from which by far the greater part of the victims were drawn, was in the deepest mourning from end to end. ... There was a short service in the church, and the interment was in the Lutheran Cemetery, Queens Borough. There was no large gathering at the church to attend this, the first of the funerals of the Slocum victims. Few seemed to realize that the time for burying had come before many had succeeded in finding their dead. Of all the persons gathered in the church — and there were nearly a hundred when the funeral took place — there were very few who were not seeking news at the bureau of information which was established, of their missing relatives or friends. The search for the missing was kept up all day long, and even while other funeral services were being held in the darkened church and the hearses were carrying the dead to the cemeteries grief-stricken men and women were begging for some word at the church door, and in the majority of instances, learning nothing, would make the journey to the Morgue and seek again among the dead, then back to the church again to see if something had not been heard there at last."

A picture of unidentified bodies being buried on June 18

THE EXCURSION STEAMER GENERAL SLOCUM, DESTROYED BY FIRE, AND BEACHED ON NORTH BROTHER ISLAND.

[Photograph by the New York Tribune.]

Pictures of the wrecked *Slocum*

Chapter 6: How Did Such a Thing Happen?

"'How did such a thing happen?' That was the question which was reiterated up and down the length and breadth of the city. People read of the captain who found at 110th street that his boat, with its precious cargo, was on fire and yet did not drive it to the shore until he was beyond 138th street, a mile and a half from the place where the cry of "Fire!" first reached his ears. Captain William H. Van Schaick of the Slocum explained, as best he could, how such horrible disaster had come to a company under his care and direction. He is a man 61 years old, and has had long experience in commanding pleasure craft in the waters around New York. Captain Van Schaick said that though he heard the alarm of fire early, he made up his mind at once that there was no certain place where she could be beached in shallow water south of North Brother Island. The tide was running up to the Sound with terrific velocity, and he was sure that he would lose time trying to turn his boat into a proper beaching place south of North Brother Island. He stuck to his post, although the flames scorched his clothing, until the boat was hard and fast ashore. Pilot Van Wart stayed with him." – J.S. Ogilvie, History of the General Slocum disaster by which nearly 1200 lives were lost by the burning of the steamer General Slocum in Hell gate, New York harbor, June 15, 1904 (1904)

Naturally, it did not take long at all for people to begin to look for reasons behind the *Slocum* tragedy, and, more importantly for many, someone to blame for their pain. In fact, the metal on the burning hulk was still smoldering when the *New York Tribune* opined, "A number of lessons will be found by wide-awake steam-boatmen in this disaster when the facts are better known than they are to-day. The chief one will relate to the prevention of any such outbreak of fire as that which occurred on the General Slocum. Another will deal with improvements in construction. In the meantime the public will do well to recognize the probability that travel on excursion boats during the remainder of the season will be safer than it was before. If no new precautions are adopted, at least a greater vigilance will be exercised. Again, the majority of the patrons of these boats also have something to learn about the safeguards provided for them by law. One person in ten, perhaps, can swim, but it is doubtful if one in a hundred can put on a life preserver. To make use of the latter in a crowd, and when a panic develops, may not be possible, but these hindrances do not always exist when the need arises. Many lives might have been saved yesterday if, before going on board the General Slocum, all of her passengers had familiarized themselves with the arrangement of a life preserver and the art of donning one in the right manner."

The New York Tribune on June 16, 1904

    Of course, knowing how to put on a life preserver does no good when they malfunction, and as word began to spread about the condition of the equipment on the ship, particularly the lifeboats and life preservers, the *New York World* complained, "That so many persons should die in broad daylight upon a crowded harbor arm without fault of unpreparedness or such emergencies is inconceivable. The crew did as much as its numbers and its obvious lack of drill would, permit. …The captain may be criticized for driving his boat a mile into the teeth of a strong wind; but his was at least a trained judgment, liable to error but doing its best at a critical moment. For the chief burden of fault we must go further. It was in the boat herself; in her rotten and useless 'life preservers;' in her scanty equipment for fighting fire; but above and beyond all else in her construction, which fitted her and others like her for a fire-trap and for nothing else. This is no new discovery. The World has already, has emphatically, has repeatedly shown the criminal absurdity of 'inspection' laws that permit the officials to examine boilers and count passengers' noses, but do not permit them to question the safety of the hull except as to seaworthiness. Perhaps, with the lesson of this frightful disaster before it. Congress may now frame the legislation that has been so long urged upon it."

The New York World on June 15, 1904

Frank Barnaby, who owned the *General Slocum*, read these articles with great concern, for if fault was found in his vessel, he could be held liable. He immediately contacted his attorneys and began to gather together documentation that made it at least appear that the life preservers were indeed in good shape and that the only problem was that people did not put them on properly.

This story began to fall apart, however, when divers began bringing the bodies to the surface. Many of them were wearing properly affixed life preservers, only to still sink to the bottom of the river just as quickly as those who had none.

Barnaby next tried to blame the inspection system, agreeing with the *World* that not enough was done to make owners aware of the deficiencies in their vessels. He painted himself as a man who wanted to do the right thing but was misinformed by Henry Lundberg, the inspector who had most recently approved the *Slocum*'s condition. The *Evening Post* supported this accusation, possibly with some encouragement from Barnaby: "The *General Slocum*, bearing the inspectors' certificate of full equipment, had no effective means of saving her own hull from fire or the life of a single passenger from drowning. …we have talked with those who drew ashore bodies actually weighted down by the life preservers that Inspector Lundberg declares in an interview were 'in good condition.' We know that these life belts, when thrown into the water, sank like stones; when ripped open displayed a mixture of soggy cork and glue, no more buoyant than so much dirt. Now, recall that the fire hose which did not work, the life-rafts which could not be released from their wire lashings, the life preservers which came to pieces when they could be reached, and dragged down the unfortunate swimmers who wore them, had all been inspected and declared not only serviceable, but of the first quality. These life-belts, which possibly had never been buoyant, bore an inspector's mark of buoyancy from the factory, and the certificate of successive inspectors that no deterioration had taken place. Inspector Lundberg, on May 5 last, certified under oath that the life preservers were 500 in excess of the legal requirement, and all in good condition. He said yesterday that he tested all "that appeared in any way old," and did not reject one."

The men in question did not have long to get their stories together, because on the Monday following the disaster, hearings were convened to determine what went wrong. Divers who had previously been searching for bodies were tasked with searching for evidence, and according to one report, "Five feet of the fire hose of the General Slocum was recovered from the wreck by Diver Tulloch, and turned over to Coroner O'Gorman to serve as evidence at the inquest. The hose was burned at both ends and on a fold in the middle, as though it had never been unreeled. The hose is a two and a half inch canvas tube without any rubber lining whatever."

The same report went on to quote one former Fire Marshal who examined the hose and said, "The rough weave of the canvas on the inside causes a considerable loss of force at the nozzle on account of the friction with the water. Roughly, in such hose as that the loss due to friction would be about forty pounds to a hundred feet of hose. The hose is porous also, and leaks somewhat. That is, it 'sweats,' causing a further loss of power, until the fiber of the hose swells and makes the coating thoroughly impervious to water. That would take about ten minutes."

The report added, "From the sunken vessel one of the starboard steel lifeboats was also brought up. The boat was still attached to the davits, to which it was lashed by steel wires instead of ropes. The boat was crumpled up in the middle, as if it had been paper, and great gaps had been sprung in its bow. But boatmen say it would have been serviceable if it had ever been got into the water."

As the investigation progressed, Captain Van Schaick became a convenient scapegoat for many. When first interviewed immediately after the incident, he told the coroner, Joseph Berry, "We left the foot of East Twenty-Third Street about 9.30 o'clock. It was reported to me that 982 tickets for adults had been taken in at the gangways. This does not include children who came aboard, or passengers who paid their fare at the gangways. I should say there were about 1,400 souls aboard when we started on the trip up the river. I took the boat slowly up the river, and we were bearing over toward the Sunken Meadows after passing through Hell Gate, when I heard shouts of 'fire.' I was in the pilot-house at the time. I sounded the alarm for fire drill. Fire apparatus was stationed on the boat and the crew had been schooled in its use. I saw smoke issuing from the companionways forward, and my first thought was that it was coming from the boiler-rooms. I swung the boat over toward North Brother Island, knowing it was the safest and quickest place to land. Response to the bell in the engine-room showed me that the engineer, B. F. Conklin, or some of his assistants, were still at their post. A few moments before the boat grounded in the channel off North Brother Island the flames were licking the pilot-house. Followed by my pilots, I ran over the deck and jumped- into the river. My hat and clothing were burning when I jumped. I reckon the time between the first alarm and when we grounded at about five minutes. I floundered in the water and do not know who pulled me out as I neared the shore. Someone dragged me up under a tree, and it was some time before I was revived. I made the quickest and best landing under the circumstances."

Later, however, the captain changed his story: "I was in the pilot-house opposite Sixty-Fourth Street and saluted the Grand republic, which passed me at that point. I then walked aft to my cabin and stood at the door for a few moments, then went in and sat down. While I was sitting down the mate sent up an alarm of fire. We were then midway between the Sunken Meadows and North Brother Island. I gave orders to go ahead, and in three minutes the boat was beached on the shore of North Brother Island. If I had turned back to the Sunken Meadows the time I would have lost would have cost the lives of all on board. If I had turned and run to the Bronx shore or any other shore the boat would have struck head on and would have bumped us again into deep water."

Within two weeks, the grand jury had indicted Van Schaick and 10 others and charged them with manslaughter. Both Lundberg and Barnaby were acquitted, though the former was tried three times. Van Schaick, however, was ultimately convicted and sentenced to 10 years of hard labor in Sing Sing. His wife, unwilling to have her husband take all the blame for the incident, devoted herself to writing letters to President Roosevelt and then President William Taft until the latter pardoned him.

As for the *Slocum* itself, its tragic story had one more interesting twist. Enough of the steamboat was salvaged so that it could be converted into a coal barge, and it subsequently sailed for seven more years before ultimately going down off the coast of Atlantic City.

The grim fates suffered by the ship and so many of its passengers may not have been fair, but then again, history rarely is.

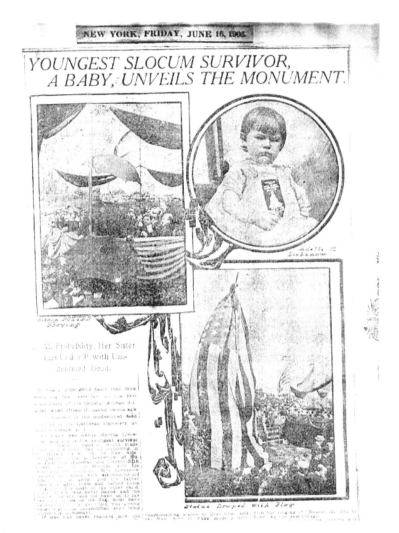

Adele Martha Liebenow, the youngest survivor of the disaster. New York Historical Society

A cartoon in the *Chicago Daily News* comparing peacetime disasters, including the *General Slocum*, to war

Memorial to the General Slocum disaster, found in Tompkins Square Park, Manhattan, New York City.

"IN MEMORY OF THOSE WHO LOST THEIR LIVES IN THE DISASTER TO THE STEAMER GENERAL SLOCUM JUNE XV MCMIV THEY WERE EARTH'S PUREST CHILDREN, YOUNG AND OLD"

Taken by Erik Edson on November 20, 2007.

Online Resources

Other titles about maritime disasters by Charles River Editors

Other titles about the General Slocum on Amazon

Bibliography

Braatz, Werner and Starr, Joseph. Fire on the River: The Story of the Burning of the General Slocum. Krokodiloplis Press, 2000. ISBN 0-9749363-0-8

Kornblum, William. *At Sea in the City: New York from the Water's Edge*

Nash, Jay. Darkest Hours. Chicago: Nelson-Hall, 1976. ISBN 0-88229-140-8

O'Donnell, Ed. Ship Ablaze: The Tragedy of the Steamboat General Slocum. Broadway, 2003. ISBN 0-7679-0905-4

Made in the USA
Monee, IL
18 August 2022